THE STARS FALL?

MAKES A RAINBOW?

WHAT GOOD ARE TAILS?

Do the rings of a tree stump tell its age?

Do flowers sleep at night?

Do ostriches bury their heads in the sand?

WHAT IS THE DIFFERENCE BETWEEN A FRUIT AND A VEGETABLE?

ARE SHELLFISH REALLY FISH?

SPONGE?

Why do leaves change color in the fall?

WHY DON'T WE FALL OFF THE EARTH?

Why do cherries and plums have pits?

SALTY?

WHAT IS FOG?

THE QUESTION AND ANSWER

★ RANDOM HOUSE ★

BOOK OF NATURE

ANIMALS ARE THE MOST INTELLIGENT?

RANDOM HOUSE · NEW YORK

THE QUESTION AND ANSWER BOOK OF NATURE

by John R. Saunders • Illustrated by Donald Moss

CONTENTS

About the Animal Kingdom

How many different kinds of animals are there?

There are more different kinds of animals than we would think possible. When we think of animals we think of our pets, the animals on a farm, the animals in a zoo and the squirrels and chipmunks that run in and out of our yards. We forget the ocean and its inhabitants. We forget insects, worms and spiders. We even forget that birds are animals.

To a scientist an animal is anything that is alive in the world but is not a plant. Therefore, we must include in our list even the one-celled animals like the amoeba. Any one kind of animal is called a species, and a species may include billions of the same kind of animals. Scientists have studied and given a name to close to a million species of animals.

Can animals think?

Certainly animals do not think as we do, but we cannot deny that their instinctive behavior is as remarkable as thinking. We have all heard of cats which have found their way back home after having been taken hundreds of miles away. A frog taken far from water will instantly find the shortest way to a stream. The building of dams by beavers, the elaborate tunnels of the ants, the ingenious nests of the birds—all these are the result of instinct, the animals' natural impulse to behave in a certain way. And yet there must be some thinking in these inborn patterns of behavior.

What animals are the most intelligent?

For a long time the chimpanzee has been considered the most intelligent animal—next to man, of course. And the chimpanzee is followed by the orangutan, the gorilla and the monkey. However, some scientists argue that the elephant is smarter than the chimpanzee or monkey. Elephants can learn many commands and even work out problems.

Of course intelligence is very difficult to determine. For example, a beaver is a remarkable dam and bridge builder but is difficult to train. Other animals have a very definite ability to be trained. We have all noticed this when we have seen a dog bring its master the morning paper.

Recently, remarkable research has been done with dolphins, and some people think that they may prove to be the most intelligent animals—equal in their own way to man. As yet, though, scientists have not completed their studies of the dolphin.

Do animals talk to each other?

Yes, animals do talk to each other, but it is "animal talk" not human talk. A mother robin coaxing her babies to try their wings is really talking, for she is getting an idea across to them. A kitten meowing to tell its mother that it is hungry is actually talking in its own way. The bark of a dog, the neigh of a horse, the baa of a lamb, the trumpeting of an elephant, all express a feeling. That feeling can be any one of a number of things such as hunger, fear, joy or anger.

Cow

Glass lizard

What good are tails?

The tails of animals are good for many things. A cow uses its tail as a fly swatter when it swishes away pesty insects. A fox wraps itself up in its tail to keep warm. A kangaroo leans on its tail as a prop. A beaver uses its flat tail to slap the water as a signal. A fish uses its tail to help it swim. A lizard sheds its tail as a protection and can then grow a new one. A squirrel uses its tail as a rudder and also as a parachute as it jumps through the treetops.

What is the largest animal?

The blue whale, also called the sulphur-bottom, is the largest animal. Some of these blue whales have reached a length of 109 feet and have weighed 150 tons. Strangely enough, these giants of the animal kingdom eat small shrimplike animals which whalers call "krill."

Flying squirrel

Kangaroo

Beaver

Red fox

How long do animals live?

A tortoise may live more than 200 years if it gets enough to eat and escapes disease and enemies. An elephant, which takes a long time to grow up, may live seventy-five or eighty years. Your dog or cat will average about ten or fifteen years, but a rat or mouse will live only two or three years. Birds vary a great deal in their length of life. A canary or a chicken may live about twenty years, but a swan, a parrot or a goose may live more than fifty years.

What animals sleep all winter?

Some animals hibernate all winter. Their heart beat, breathing and digestion slow down, and their bodies become very cold. These winter sleepers include the ground squirrels, woodchucks, some bats and jumping mice. Other animals like the bear, skunk, chipmunk and badger sleep part of the winter but will come out during mild weather. Many toads, turtles, snakes, frogs and salamanders and some insects also hibernate.

A blue whale, the largest living animal

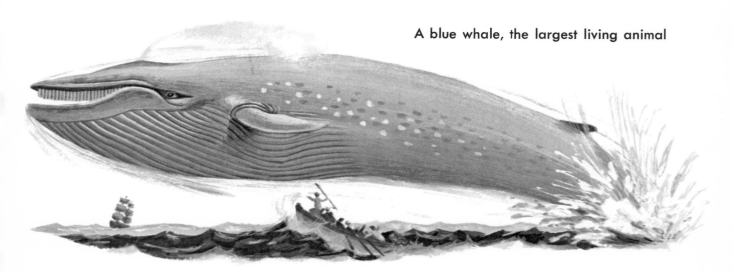

Why do the eyes of some animals shine in the dark?

The eyes of some animals, especially cats, seem to glow in the dark. But actually they are simply reflecting light. At the back of a cat's eyes is a special layer of cells that acts as a mirror. It picks up whatever light there is and reflects it. Cats cannot see in complete darkness, as many people believe, but they *can* see in a very dim light. This is because the iris—the colored circle around the pupil in their eyes—opens wide to let in every bit of light possible, enabling them to see better. This is also the reason why a cat's eyes look so big when they glow in the dark.

What animal can run the fastest?

The cheetah, or hunting leopard of India, can run faster than any other four-legged animal. It has been clocked at seventy miles an hour. Some other interesting speeds are: a deer at fifty miles an hour, a horse at forty miles an hour, a vulture flying at eighty-nine miles an hour and a golden eagle at about one hundred and twenty miles an hour.

INVERTEBRATES: WITHOUT BACKBONES

Is the jellyfish a fish?

Though it is a sea animal, the jellyfish is not a fish. Fishes are animals with backbones, but the so-called jellyfish has a thick saucer-shaped body that looks like jelly. Around its edges are many fringes and ruffles. These fringes contain thousands of stinging cells. The sting of the common small jellyfish is unpleasant but not dangerous.

What are night crawlers?

Night crawlers are earthworms. During the day earthworms burrow underground, but at night they come up to the surface. Fishermen often collect them to use as bait in catching fish.

Can a worm live when it is cut in two?

Yes, a worm can live when it is cut in two. This is possible because a worm doesn't have a brain as we do. In man and in most animals if the brain is severely injured, death results. In worms a nervous system which is spread throughout the body takes the place of a brain. Therefore, when a worm is injured or part of its body is cut off, the loss is not great enough to cause death.

Not only does the worm stay alive, but it can actually grow a new part if not more than half of the body is lost. Man cannot grow a new arm or leg, but certain lower animals can. This ability to grow a new part is called *regeneration*.

What is a sponge?

Most sponges used today are synthetic (man-made) sponges which imitate the natural sponge. The natural sponge is really the soft elastic skeleton of an animal that lives in the sea. Since this sea animal has no legs, fins or stomach and does not move around at all, people did not know for many years that it is an animal and not a plant.

Are shellfish really fish?

No, shellfish are not really fish. Shellfish are animals such as crabs, lobsters, barnacles and shrimp whose hard outer covering we call a shell. These soft-bodied animals with hard shells should properly be called *crustaceans*. Another group of hard-shelled animals are also often referred to as shellfish. These are the *mollusks*, and they include clams, oysters and scallops. Neither the mollusks nor the crustaceans are related to fish. Fish have backbones; mollusks and crustaceans do not.

Can we hear the sea in a sea shell?

When we hold a large spiral-shaped shell to our ear we hear a roar, but it is not the roar of the sea. The shell magnifies faint sound vibrations in the air. The shape of the shell and the smooth inner side make the noises echo back and forth. Sounds that we may not normally hear are picked up by the shell and made louder. It is rather fun to think that this noise is the roar of the sea, even though we know that it isn't.

How does an oyster make a pearl?

Sometimes a little grain of sand or some other tiny object will get inside the shell of a sea pearl oyster. This irritates the soft body of the oyster. As a protection it coats the sand with layer after layer of the same glowing substance it makes to line its shell. We call this substance mother-of-pearl. Gradually the particle of sand is wrapped in so many layers that a little ball forms. This ball is a pearl.

Years ago it was found that grains of sand could be "planted" inside the oyster shells to encourage them to make pearls. Pearls produced by this method are called cultured pearls, and they are less valuable than those which grow naturally. The oysters we eat are not the oysters that produce valuable pearls. The pearls of edible oysters are dull and do not gleam.

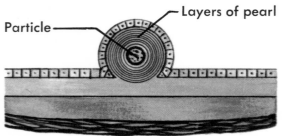

Particle

Layers of pearl

CROSS SECTION OF OYSTER SHELL AND PEARL

INSECTS AND ARACHNIDS

Are insects of any use to us?

Some insects are very useful indeed. Butterflies and bees, for instance, carry the yellow dust called pollen from one flower to another. This transfer of pollen makes it possible for plants to grow seeds. Bees also give us honey, and from the cocoon of silk worms we get silk for our clothing.

Of course there are also many harmful insects which spread disease, damage plants, and eat clothing and furniture. And there are insects like the mosquito that bite us. But in spite of all these insect pests, we should remember that vast numbers of insects are harmless and many are truly helpful. The praying mantis and the ladybird beetle even eat large numbers of the harmful insects. In that way they help us to control the damage done by insect pests.

What is a praying mantis?

The praying mantis is an insect. It is from two to five inches long, depending on the kind. And it is green or brown in color. The praying mantis, or mantid, is related to the grasshoppers and crickets. Its strange name comes from its habit of holding its two front legs folded as though they were arms. In this position it looks exactly as though it were praying. Actually it is not praying at all, but waiting for flies, mosquitoes, beetles and grasshoppers to pounce on and eat. It should be named "preying"

mantis, for it snatches its prey with fierce speed.

In wintertime, it is fun to look for the brownish egg cases of praying mantises. They are about as big as walnuts. In the spring about 200 babies will hatch out.

How can a fly walk on the ceiling without falling off?

A fly can walk upside down on the ceiling because of the pads on each of its six feet. If you look at a fly with a magnifying glass, you can see these pads clearly. Some scientists think that a sticky substance on the pads holds the fly to the ceiling. Others who have studied the fly believe that the hollow pads flatten out against the surface and hold on by suction.

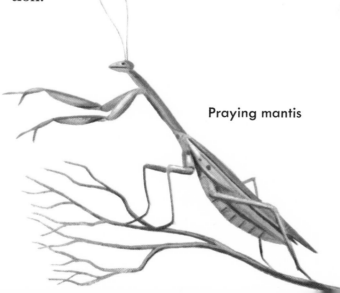

Praying mantis

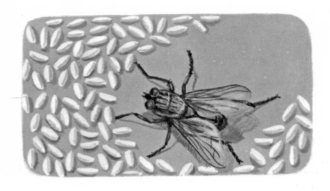

Do flies lay eggs?

Yes, flies certainly do lay eggs. These eggs are laid in batches of about 125 each. And one female housefly may lay as many as 21 batches during her lifetime—more than 2500 eggs! They hatch in a matter of hours if the weather is warm, and in about three days if the weather is cool.

The eggs hatch into little white worms called maggots. Then, like butterflies, they have a resting stage—called a pupal stage. During the pupal stage they change from a little worm to a fly with wings. This change takes about five days. There may be as many as ten generations of flies born in one year. This means that one female may have trillions of descendants born during the period between April and September. Since flies carry disease, it is important to destroy their breeding places, usually places of filth.

Where do flies go in the winter?

Most flies die in the winter, but a very few may happen to find a crack and stay there until the warm sun of spring makes them active again. However, the cold weather does not kill off the pupal stage of the fly. During this period, the wormlike pupa has a hard, protective shell around it and does not move all winter. When warm weather arrives, a grown fly with wings comes out of the shell. The change has taken place gradually, just as a caterpillar turns into a butterfly inside its hard case, called a chrysalis.

How do fireflies light up?

Fireflies produce two chemical juices, luciferin and luciferase, in their bodies. When these juices mix with oxygen, they give off light. However, this light does not produce heat; instead, it is a cool light. Scientists are not certain why fireflies make this light. It is thought to be a signal to attract a mate.

How do bees make honey?

Bees gather a sweet liquid called nectar from flowers. They store this nectar in their "honey stomach" until they can return to the hive. The honey stomach is not the same stomach that the bee uses to digest its food. It is a special stomach where the nectar is mixed with chemicals secreted by glands in the bee.

When the bee returns to the hive, it sucks the nectar back up from the honey stomach. The nectar is then placed in the honeycomb. Here the water in the nectar quickly disappears and the chemicals secreted inside the bee turn the nectar into honey.

How dangerous is the sting of a bee or a wasp?

Usually when people are stung by a bee or wasp, the sting causes sudden pain and there may be some swelling. This is normal, and after a while the pain becomes less uncomfortable. Some people, however, are extremely sensitive to bee stings. Severe reactions or even death may result. A doctor should be called at once if there are serious symptoms, such as swelling of the eyes and lips, a rash over the entire body or general weakness. If you are stung by a bee, it is always wise to scrape off the stinger right away. Then less poison will be able to enter the wound.

Does a bee die when it stings you?

Yes, most bees do die when they sting you. The reason for this is that the stinger is barbed or hooked. It remains stuck in your flesh, and soft parts of the bee's body pull off with the stinger. The loss of these parts soon proves fatal to the bee. The exception is the queen bee, whose stinger is curved and smooth. The queen can use her stinger over and over again without harmful results. However, we need not fear her, for she uses her stinger only on other queens.

Moth

What is the difference between a moth and a butterfly?

Moths usually fly at night and butterflies fly during the day. When a moth lands on a twig, it usually holds its wings out straight or horizontal. When a butterfly lands on a twig, it holds its wings upright or vertical. The body of a moth is thick and hairy; the body of a butterfly is slender and not hairy. The antennae of a butterfly have clublike knobs at the ends; those of the moth lack these knobs. The antennae of the moth are often feathery, like tiny plumes. Those of a butterfly are usually threadlike.

Butterfly

How long do butterflies live?

This is a difficult question to answer. We know that some butterflies live for only a few days. Others live for only a few weeks. Yet there are some kinds of butterflies that sleep through the winter, hidden in places where they are sheltered from bad weather. The monarch butterfly, like the robin, migrates to warmer regions in the autumn. Sometimes these traveling butterflies fly together in great winged clouds.

What is a cocoon?

A cocoon is a protective case made by an insect. The insect in its pupal form lives inside the cocoon while changing into its adult form. Most moth caterpillars make cocoons from silk glands in their bodies. The cocoons are usually attached to branches or twigs. Inside, the caterpillar sheds its skin and becomes a pupa, which slowly changes to a winged moth.

How does a caterpillar turn into a butterfly?

When a caterpillar is fully grown it stops eating. Wiggling along the stem of a plant, it fastens itself to the underside of a twig by a loop of silken thread and a small button or pad of silk. Then it sheds its skin for the last time as a caterpillar. Underneath is another skin which stiffens and becomes a hard case called a chrysalis.

For weeks or months this chrysalis or

pupa lies motionless. But inside many changes are slowly taking place. First the body of the caterpillar turns into a creamy liquid. Then four wings, six legs, antennae and new and different eyes begin to form. Spring comes and the covering splits open. A butterfly with tiny, damp wings struggles out. It hangs on a twig and gradually its wings expand and dry. Soon it is ready to fly off in search of nectar-filled flowers.

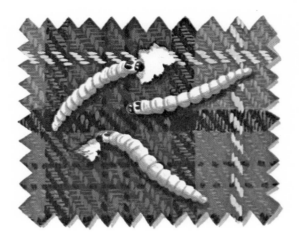

Why do moths eat our clothes?

Certain moths eat our clothes for nourishment. They like wool and hair particularly. Of course it's not the adult moth with wings that does the eating. It is the caterpillar of the moth before it gets its wings. The hungry moth caterpillar has a mouth well suited for chewing. The adult moth with wings can't chew anything, for its mouth is suitable only for sucking. And some adult moths do not eat at all. The food of adult moths is usually the sweet liquid called nectar found in flowers.

Can caterpillars sting?

Not all caterpillars are able to sting us, but a few can. The caterpillar of the Io moth, for example, is covered with poisonous spines that sting and burn when they pierce the skin. Others are covered with hairs which give off a poison that irritates our skin and makes it smart.

Silkworm moth and eggs

Young larvae

Older larvae

Larvae spinning cocoons

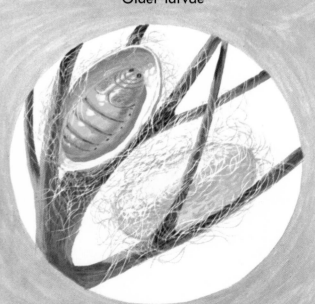

Open cocoon showing pupa

Adult moth

How does a silkworm give us silk?

The silkworm, of course, makes silk for itself—not for us. It spins its cocoon of silk as a protective case in which it can change from a silkworm into a moth. The silkworm is really a caterpillar, the larval stage of the silk moth.

The silk, in the form of a thick liquid, comes from two glands in the body of the silkworm. As the gluelike liquid comes out of the mouth, it hardens into a thread. One of these threads is often as much as 1,000 feet long. The worm winds the thread around and around its body, forming a cocoon. Many years ago the Chinese learned how to unravel these cocoons and weave the long silk threads into cloth.

What is a seventeen-year locust?

The seventeen-year locust is not a true locust at all. True locusts are grasshoppers. The seventeen-year locust belongs to the cicada family, and it is the most common kind of cicada found in America. It lives most of its life underground in the form of a little grub or nymph. There it feeds on root juices, taking either thirteen or seventeen years to develop into an adult.

When it is ready to emerge, the seventeen-year locust digs its way to the surface and climbs a tree. There it cracks open its skin and crawls out, dries off its new wings and flies away. It lives only a short time as an adult—long enough to mate and lay eggs.

Are ladybugs useful?

Yes, ladybugs are useful. They are useful because they eat large quantities of aphids, the fuzzy plant lice that eat our crops. These ladybugs or ladybird beetles are so useful that they were collected in large numbers along the Pacific Coast and then let go in areas where crops were being eaten by aphids.

Are "darning needles" harmful?

When people speak of "darning needles," they are actually talking about dragonflies. And they are usually surprised to learn that these beautiful insects are absolutely harmless. Not only are they harmless, but they are also very valuable for they eat many harmful insects such as flies and mosquitoes. The dragonfly has special eyes, each one made up of about 25,000 tiny eyes all joined together. Because of these eyes, it can see other insects extremely well—long before they have a chance to get out of the way.

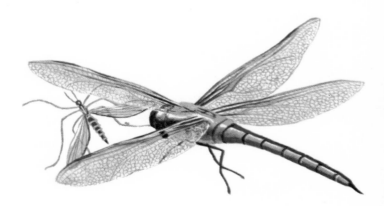

How does a cricket chirp?

Crickets chirp by rubbing their wings together. Each of their front wings has a kind of double file and scraper on it. The file is a thickened vein with cross-ridges, while the scraper is a kind of sharp-edged, toothed part. When the scraper of one wing is rubbed across the file of the other wing, a chirping sound is made. The sound is amplified or made louder by a "sounding board." This sounding board is a space free of veins in the center of each wing. Only male crickets chirp.

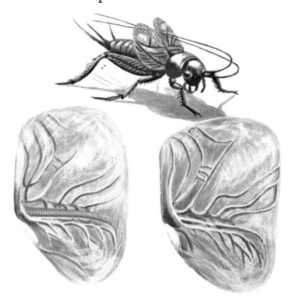

What are the little white objects that ants carry?

These little white objects are ant cocoons. They are often mistakenly called ant eggs, but real ant eggs are much tinier. Sometimes we see ants carrying tiny wormlike creatures. These are the larvae just after they have hatched from the eggs and before they have spun their little cocoons or cases. In their cocoons they change from little worms to ants, just as a caterpillar changes into a butterfly or moth. Ant cocoons are gathered and sold as food for turtles, fish and birds.

What is a daddy-longlegs?

A daddy-longlegs is not an insect, for it has eight legs instead of six. It is a creature related to the spiders, but it does not spin a web. It is easily recognized by its tiny body and extremely long thread-like legs. If it loses a leg, it will grow a new one! It is interesting to capture a daddy-longlegs, put it under a glass, feed it sweetened water, and observe it awhile before letting it go.

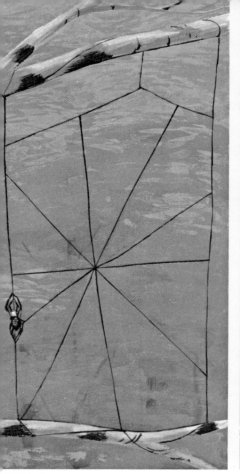
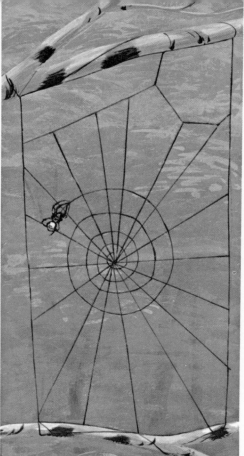

How does a spider spin a web?

A spider, which is classified as an *arachnid* rather than an insect, weaves its web from a kind of liquid silk produced inside the spider's own body. This liquid hardens into a silklike thread when drawn outside the body. At the hind end of the spider's body are three pairs of remarkable spinning organs called spinnerets. As the liquid silk is drawn out of the body, the spinnerets combine the fine threads into thicker strands. Some of the strands are coated with a sticky substance.

One of the most familiar kinds of spider webs is the orb web. It looks like a wheel with spokes. The orb-weaver spider usually fastens its web quite high off the ground—perhaps on a tree or plant. Using its hind leg, the spider draws a thread from its spinnerets. This thread dangles in the air until it sticks to a branch, twig or some other object. After the spider has anchored and strengthened this "bridge" line, it spins the rest of the framework and adds the "spokes." The final addition is the long continuous spinal line that runs from spoke to spoke in a circular or spiral pattern. This spiral line is sticky and holds the insects that are caught for food.

A spider is careful to walk only on the dry threads it spins. But even if it should slip and touch the sticky threads, it would not be caught for its body has an oily covering.

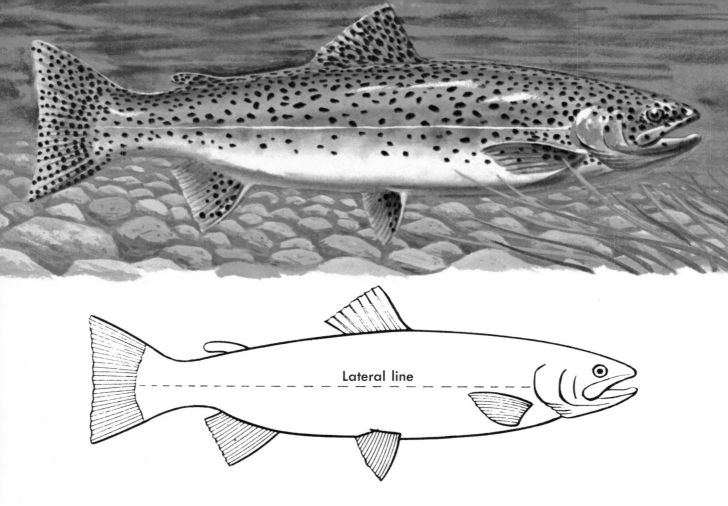

Lateral line

FISH

How can a fish breathe in water?

Both fish and men need oxygen in order to live. They take in this oxygen when they breathe. But men obtain their oxygen from the air, while fish get theirs from water.

On each side of the throat of most fish there are slits called gill openings. The gills themselves are breathing organs located in hollow places inside the fish's body. When a fish breathes, it opens its mouth and takes in water. The water is then forced over the gills and out through the gill slits. The oxygen in the water is absorbed by tiny blood vessels in the gills and carried by the blood to other parts of the body.

Can fish hear?

Fish have ears which are deep inside their heads—not outside as ours are. Their hearing is not keen, though they are aware of many sounds. Along each side of most fish runs a line of special scales. This row of scales is called the *lateral line*. A tiny hole in each scale opens into a long canal that runs from head to tail. Special organs in this canal catch sounds and send them through nerves to the brain. Because of this lateral line, we sometimes say that fish have a sixth sense. It makes them aware of danger and very quick to dart away if there is a loud noise or if an object comes near them.

Why do we put plants in a fish tank?

Plants growing in a fish tank give off oxygen. Fish need oxygen in order to live. Of course oxygen is already present in the water, but plants increase the supply and help keep the fish healthy. In return, fish give off carbon dioxide, a gas that plants use to make their own food.

Plants also provide landscaping and a natural environment for fish.

Do fish shut their eyes, or sleep?

Fish have no eyelids. Therefore they cannot close their eyes and go to sleep as we do. There is no doubt, however, that fish rest at the bottom of a pond or a river or an aquarium, even though they do not sleep in the usual way.

Is a shark a fish?

Yes, a shark is a fish. It is a simple and primitive fish. Instead of having a bony skeleton, a shark has a skeleton of cartilage (gristle). Its hide is tough with small rough toothlike scales.

How can fish live in a frozen pond?

If we mean a pond that is frozen solid from top to bottom, then fish can *not* live there. Solid ice will not give them the oxygen they need to keep alive. But usually when we talk about a frozen pond we mean one with just a covering of ice. This sheet of ice has water below it, and a fresh supply of oxygen is usually provided by water that flows into the pond below the ice. At the edge of the pond there are also apt to be holes in the ice. These let in oxygen, too.

How fast can fish swim?

A salmon can swim at a speed of seven miles an hour and a pike at ten miles an hour. The wahoo, a large mackerel type of tropical game fish, can swim at a speed of thirty miles an hour, and a flying fish at thirty-five miles an hour. This indicates that there is great variation in speed among the various fish.

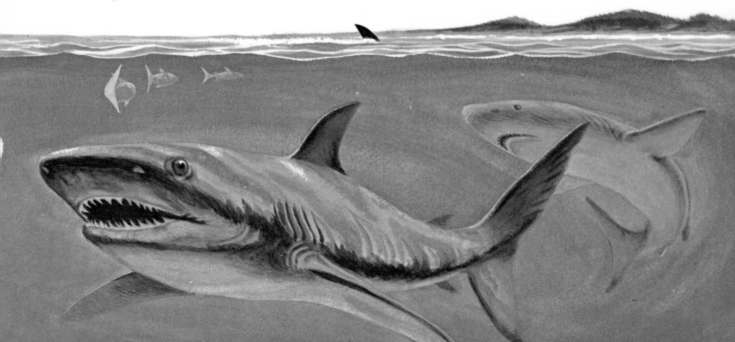

AMPHIBIANS:
ANIMALS THAT MOVE FROM WATER TO LAND

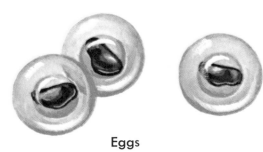

Eggs

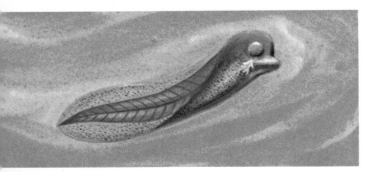

Newly hatched tadpole

Tadpole with legs and tail

Frog with tail almost gone

Where does the tadpole's tail go when the tadpole becomes a frog?

A tadpole—or a "pollywog" as it is sometimes called—looks very much like a fish. It has a tail and it breathes with gills. But unlike a fish, the tadpole will start to show wonderful changes as it eats and grows larger. Legs and lungs will begin to grow. And the gills will begin to shrink.

One day the tadpole will come to the top of the water and take a sniff of air instead of breathing with its gills. As it continues to sniff the air, its lungs will get larger and its gills will get smaller. Finally the gills will disappear altogether.

While this is taking place, the tail seems to be getting smaller and smaller. It does not drop off, but it is slowly absorbed by the body as the frog tadpole sprouts a pair of hind legs, then a pair of front legs.

Toad tadpoles change in much the same way. But the adult toads do not go back to the water until they are ready to lay eggs, whereas most kinds of frogs stay near water all of their lives.

What do frogs eat?

Fortunately for us, frogs eat mosquitoes. They also eat flies, moths, beetles, small crayfish and worms. A frog's mouth is very large with two rows of teeth on the upper jaw only. It has a long, sticky tongue attached to the front, not the back, of its mouth. This tongue can be flipped out to catch insects as "quick as a wink."

Do people really eat frogs' legs?

Yes, many people enjoy eating frogs' legs. The large hind legs or jumping legs are the ones used. They are usually fried in butter and are held in the fingers when eaten, just as we sometimes hold a chicken leg. In most French restaurants frogs' legs are found on the menu. There are even frog farms where frogs are raised to supply the demand for this unusual but tasty dish.

Can we get warts from toads?

No, we cannot get warts from toads. That is just a superstition. The rough skin of toads looks as if it is covered with warts, but these wartlike lumps can do us no harm. In fact toads, like frogs, do a great deal of good by eating many harmful insect pests.

Where do salamanders live?

The salamander is usually a small animal, with a lizard-like body. Like frogs and toads, salamanders are *amphibians*, animals that live part of their lives in water and part on land.

The newt is one of the most common salamanders in the United States. We often find it in the woodlands in summer, particularly after a shower. This soft-bodied little newt starts life in the water. It takes in oxygen through feathery external gills. These gills are absorbed as the newt starts its land stage during which time it is bright orange

Salamander: water stage

and is known as an "eft." Finally the newt turns a darkish green color and returns to the water to lay its eggs.

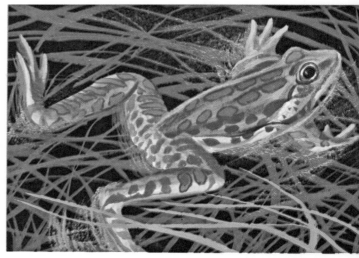

Leopard frog

Tree toad

Salamander: land stage

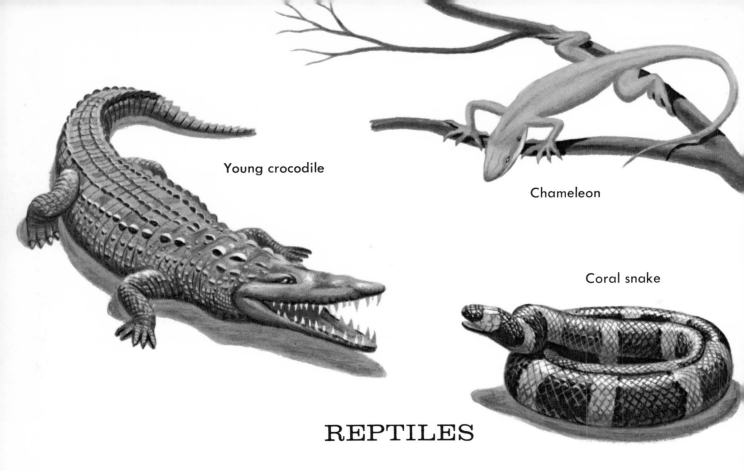

Young crocodile

Chameleon

Coral snake

REPTILES

Are snakes useful to us in any way?

Snakes are useful because they eat rats, mice and insects—pests that eat millions of dollars' worth of valuable crops each year and also spread harmful diseases. We are glad to have snakes help us get rid of them. Of course snakes eat young birds and beneficial frogs and toads, too, but the good that snakes do more than makes up for the bad.

Snake skin is cured and used in making ladies' handbags and shoes. Much of the so-called "lizard skin" is really snake skin. Rattlesnake meat is sold in cans as a food delicacy.

How can snakes move without legs?

A snake uses its ribs, as well as the scales underneath its body, to glide along the ground. The long backbone of the snake is really a chain of small bones or vertebrae. Each vertebra is fastened to a pair of ribs, and each pair of ribs is attached to one of the platelike scales that cover the underside of the snake.

The snake uses its muscles to move the ribs and the long row of scales almost as if they were a kind of feet. It is hard for a snake to crawl on a smooth flat surface, for its scales need to be able to press against uneven places in the ground.

Why does a snake shed its skin?

As a snake grows, its skin gets too small and tight for it. A new skin grows under the old one. Then when the snake is ready to shed its old skin, it rubs its nose against something rough, like a rock. This breaks the skin around the jaws and starts it peeling backward. The snake crawls out of the old skin in much the same way we often take off a tight glove—by turning it inside out as we pull it off.

Snakes may shed their skins three or four times a year, and each time the snake grows a little larger. Because young snakes grow faster than older snakes, they shed their skins more often.

Can we tell the age of a rattlesnake by counting its rattles?

No, we cannot tell the age of a rattlesnake by counting the rings or segments in its rattle. A rattlesnake is born with a soft "button" on the tip of its tail. As the snake grows it keeps shedding its skin. Each time it sheds its skin it adds a ring or segment to the rattle above the button. But since we do not know how many times a year the snake has shed its skin, we are unable to tell the age of the rattlesnake by counting the rings of its rattle.

When a snake crawls over rough rocks, some or all of the rattle segments may be broken off or shed. This is another reason why it is impossible to figure out the snake's age from its rattle.

Can snakes swim?

Yes, snakes can swim. The common water snake is a particularly good swimmer. It uses its muscles to move its body along with a kind of side-to-side wriggle. Of course snakes hold their heads out of water and breathe air, but they can also hold their breath and stay under water for quite a long time.

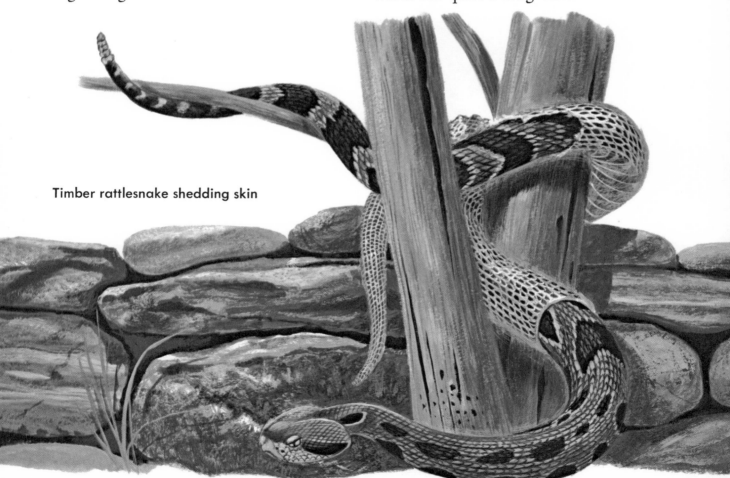

Timber rattlesnake shedding skin

Skull of nonpoisonous snake

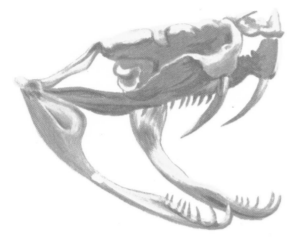

Skull of poisonous snake showing fangs

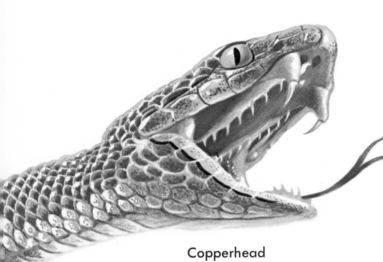

Copperhead

Is the snake's tongue a stinger?

The snake's forked tongue is not a stinger but a feeler. It acts as the snake's organ of touch. A snake also picks up particles with its tongue. These are placed in tiny cavities in the roof of the mouth where the snake does its smelling. It has two nostrils but these are used only for breathing, not for smelling.

The tongue of the snake, then, is absolutely harmless.

Is a snake's fang a tooth?

Yes, a snake's fang is a tooth, but it is a special kind of tooth which only poisonous snakes have. These teeth are hollow with tiny holes at the bottom. When the snake bites, a poison called venom is forced from a sac in the cheek through the hollow fang and into the victim. The rattler, copperhead and water moccasin fold their two fangs back against the top of the mouth when they are not in use.

Why do snakes stare at you?

Snakes appear to stare because they have no eyelids. Their eyes are always open, even when they are resting or hibernating. They do, however, have transparent shields over their eyes to protect them.

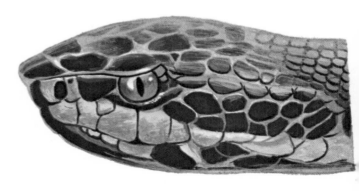

Do mother snakes swallow their young to protect them?

No, mother snakes do not swallow their young. This is just a superstition which lingers on even though it is absolutely untrue.

Can a turtle crawl out of its shell?

No, a turtle cannot crawl out of the shell that covers its short broad body above and below. This shell is really the greater part of a turtle's skeleton. The top of the shell is firmly attached to the turtle's flattened ribs which support it like the rafters of a roof. The ribs and backbone are joined into a solid mass by many bonelike plates covered by horny shields.

Sometimes we do find empty turtle shells. These are actually the skeletal remains of turtles which have died.

Can you tell the age of a turtle by its shell?

Yes, you can get a very good idea of a young turtle's age by studying its shell. A turtle's back is made up of bony plates covered by horny sections known as shields. If you look at one of these shields you will see little rings. In a young turtle each ring stands for a year's growth. After five or ten years, however, this method is no longer reliable. The edges of the shields are worn smooth, and the rings become crowded or worn off.

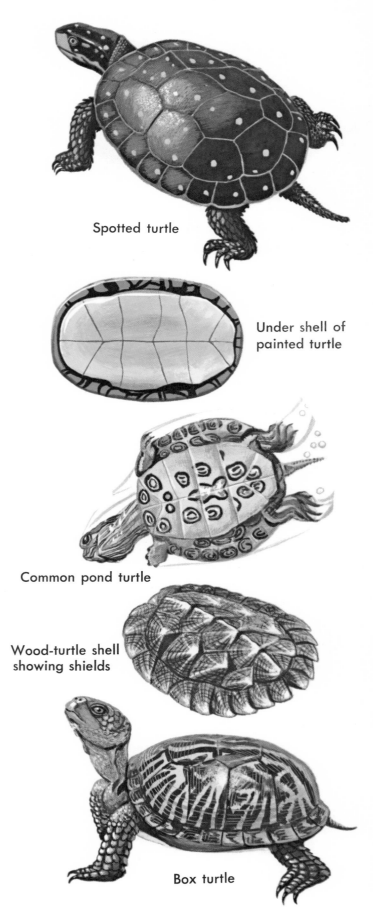

Spotted turtle

Under shell of painted turtle

Common pond turtle

Wood-turtle shell showing shields

Box turtle

BIRDS

How can birds fly?

Just as an airplane is "lifted" into the air by the swift current of air passing over the tops of the wings, a bird is able to fly because of the air rushing over its wings. When the bird moves its wings forward and down, the air is forced to move faster over the curved top surface of the wings than it moves over the narrower bottom surface. Thus the pressure on top of the wing is less than that below. The greater pressure from below gives the bird its lift.

The bird's feathers are a help too, for they are pressed tightly together on the downbeat, permitting no air to pass through them. On the upward stroke they fluff out and open up, letting the air slip through easily so the bird's flight will not be slowed down. Of course a bird is wonderfully suited for flying with its strong wing and breast muscles and its light body filled with air passages and pockets.

How fast do birds fly?

A speed of about twenty to thirty miles per hour is common for small land birds. Ducks and geese fly a bit faster—perhaps forty or fifty miles per hour. The swifts, as one might guess from the name, seem to hold the championship for speed. They fly at a rate of more than 100 miles per hour, and they have been timed at a speed of 200 miles an hour. The only bird that can challenge the swift is the duck hawk. These birds soar high in the sky to spot their prey and then seem to fall suddenly, perhaps 2,000 feet, out of the clouds. They have been clocked at 180 miles per hour as they swoop down.

Can all birds fly?

No, all birds cannot fly even though they all have two wings. The chicken cannot fly very well. It merely flutters about the barnyard. But ostriches cannot fly at all, even though they are champion runners. An ostrich may weigh between two and three hundred pounds and stand seven to eight feet tall. Flying would be very difficult for such a large bird. Among other birds which cannot fly are the penguins, the kiwis of New Zealand and the emus of Australia. The famous dodo probably disappeared because it could not fly and therefore could not escape its enemies. Unlike the ostrich it could not even run fast.

What is the largest bird in the world?

The ostrich is the largest bird in the world. It sometimes grows to a height of eight feet and weighs between two and three hundred pounds. But an ostrich cannot fly. The flying bird with the greatest wingspread is the wandering albatross. The outstretched wings of the albatross may measure as much as eleven feet from tip to tip.

Do ostriches bury their heads in the sand?

No, ostriches do not bury their heads in the sand. This ancient belief may have come about because baby ostriches often fall on the ground and stretch out their long necks when they are frightened. This largest of all birds cannot fly and therefore does need protection, but burying its head is not the answer. The ostrich's protection from danger lies in its very powerful legs and its ability to run. An ostrich can run at speeds of about forty miles an hour.

Can a hummingbird stand still in the air?

The hummingbird moves its wings so swiftly that they hum as loudly as those of a fly or bee. This rapid wing movement also makes it possible for a hummingbird to "stand still" in the air while it sucks nectar from flowers. These tiny jewel-like birds move their wings as fast as fifty or sixty strokes a second, so rapidly that our eyes see them only as a filmy haze.

Robin

Where do birds get the material to make their nests?

Birds get the materials to make their nests from plants, animals and from the soil. They collect bits of twigs, dry grass, leaves, vines, thistledown, tiny rootlets and soft inner bark from trees. They search for animal hair, soft string and stray strands of knitting yarn. In fact, if you leave colored yarn out for birds, they will almost always use it. Some birds plaster their nests with bits of mud, and some line them with their own feathers.

Thick-billed murre

Do all birds use nests?

No, not all birds use nests. Many shore birds lay their eggs right on the soft sand. The tan color of the eggs blends with the color of the sand. This protects the eggs by making them hard to discover.

Certain marine birds such as auks and murres live on rocky islands in the north and lay their eggs on a little shelf of rock. Their eggs are very pointed, so that they pivot or spin around when pushed. This keeps the eggs from rolling off the rocky ledge.

There are also lazy birds like the cuckoo and cowbird that place their eggs in the nests of other species, so that their young are brought up by foster parents.

Why do birds use birdhouses?

Certain birds like to make their nests in holes rather than on the branches of trees and shrubs. Among these are bluebirds, house wrens, chicadees, flickers, tree swallows, nuthatches and screech owls. For these birds a birdhouse is a ready-made home. It saves them the trouble of looking for a hole or of chiseling one for themselves. Once they discover the birdhouse, they busily search for twigs and grasses to line the inside. When it is sufficiently soft and comfortable, they lay their eggs and raise their family.

Robin

Bobolink

Bluejay

Red-headed
woodpecker

Crow

Does each species of bird always sing the same song?

Yes, each species usually sings the same songs—with regional variations. All robins sound like robins; all bobolinks sound like bobolinks. Most species of birds have songs and calls quite distinct and different from those of all other species. Once you know the call, you can tell what bird is singing, even though you cannot see it. One particular bird, however, may have several characteristic songs and calls. It may have different kinds of angry cries uttered when a cat or squirrel is in sight, or long low squeaks when a crow or hawk is seen, or even a variation of its own regular song.

Mockingbirds, as their name implies, are able to imitate calls and songs of other bird species, though they also have their own characteristic songs.

Why does a woodpecker peck a tree?

A woodpecker pecks a tree to get food. It eats the wood-boring insects which are just underneath the bark. Its long, barbed tongue can reach into holes and catch the insects. Most woodpeckers also chisel out nesting holes in trees. These holes are frequently used by other birds after the woodpeckers have left.

Male woodpeckers often use their bills to produce a kind of song. They make this familiar drumlike song by striking their bill with unbelievable speed against the bark of a tree, a dead branch or telephone pole.

Where do birds go in the winter?

Most birds fly south in the winter and come back again in the spring. We call this *migration*. The champion traveler is the arctic tern, which divides its time between the arctic and antarctic regions. It visits each region during the period of continuous daylight. Scientists do not know the exact reason why birds migrate. Food supply and temperature seem to play a part. The amount of daylight each day may tell them when it is time to start their trip.

Not all birds migrate. In a single neighborhood there may be permanent bird residents, summer residents and winter residents. Those which we see briefly as they pass through are called "transients."

Do birds come back to the same place year after year?

Yes, in many instances birds come back to the very same apple tree in the very same backyard year after year. This has been proved by banding the bird—placing a little metal numbered band on a bird's leg and looking to see if it's the same one when the bird returns the following season to build its nest.

Are hawks harmful?

As a whole hawks do more good than harm. They do good by eating large numbers of rats, mice and insects. These are pests that do great damage to grain crops, birds and fruit trees. There are, however, several kinds of hawks which sometimes kill chickens and game birds. Farmers and sportsmen don't like them for this reason.

Are owls really wise?

Owls are not any wiser than many other birds. In fact ravens, crows and geese are all more intelligent than owls. But owls have probably gotten a reputation for wisdom because of their large eyes and solemn expressions. A more accurate reputation would be one of usefulness. An owl is believed to be worth about twenty dollars a year to a farmer on account of the large number of rats and mice it eats.

Why does an owl come out only at night?

Certain animals are night animals just as others seem to be day animals. Most species of owls happen to be night animals. For this reason we seldom see them in the daytime, though we often hear their shrieks and hoots and know they are near by. As twilight falls, owls start their search for food—rats, mice, insects and sometimes other birds. Although owls can see in the daytime, their sight is very keen at night.

Do canaries come from the Canary Islands?

Yes, canaries did come originally from the Canary Islands off the west coast of Africa. In the beginning of the sixteenth century they were taken to Europe, and now they are found in homes throughout the world. The plumage of the wild canary is dull green. In captivity it is usually yellow, although sometimes it is reddish or orange. In America the beautiful goldfinch is often called a wild canary.

What is a homing pigeon?

A homing pigeon is a variety of domestic pigeon bred for its ability to find its way home. Years ago, before we had telephones and good methods of communication, these birds were used to carry messages which were tied to their legs. Many years of breeding and training are necessary to develop these pigeons. The young are taken a short distance from home at feeding time so that they are anxious to get back and eat. The distance is gradually increased to five miles, then ten miles, then twenty and up to fifty miles or more. As the distances get longer, fewer birds are able to find their way back home. Those that do are very special, and are bred for that purpose.

How can ducks sit in the water without getting their feathers wet?

Ducks' feathers do not get wet in the water because they are covered with an oil which makes them waterproof. Near the duck's tail is an oil gland. The duck reaches back to this gland, gets some of the oil in its bill, and then spreads the oil over its feathers. This act is called *preening*.

MAMMALS

Is a bat a bird?

No, bats are mammals—animals that feed their young with milk from the mother's body. However, bats are the only mammals that can truly fly.

Where do bats go in the daytime?

Bats are rarely seen, for they sleep all day and become active only at night. They find a sheltered spot — under the eaves of houses or barns, under a porch roof, or in a hollow tree. Caves are also a favorite spot for a daytime sleep. At twilight large numbers of bats fly out of the caves to look for food. They are so numerous they look like a dark cloud instead of bats.

Bats can see with their small eyes, but not very well. And since they are night animals and feed on flying insects, they must be able to make quick turns and dives. To make up for their lack of perfect sight, bats make high-pitched squeaks. The sound waves from these squeaks bounce off nearby objects and send back echoes to the bat's large ears. The echoes tell the bats in what direction they must fly in order not to bump into other objects or each other. In other words, bats guide their flights by sounds.

The squeaks are too high-pitched to be heard by the human ear, but they have been recorded by very sensitive machines.

How does a beaver make a dam?

Beavers have four very sharp front teeth —two in each jaw. With these teeth they can gnaw through the trunk of a tree that is two feet thick. They use the trees they cut down to make their dams and homes.

In starting a dam, the beavers select a narrow part of a stream. Then they cut down trees, trimming off the branches and cutting both tree trunks and branches into pieces of the necessary length and size. Next they drag or float the logs and branches to the spot where the dam is to be built. It is built from the bottom up, starting with logs anchored firmly with mud and stones. The cracks are filled in with both branches and mud. Beavers carry the mud in their front paws as they swim through the water.

Often several beavers work together on a dam, building it in a few nights. It may be eight feet thick at the bottom and four or five feet high. After the dam is finished, the beavers start building homes or lodges in the water behind the dam. These too are made of sticks and mud. Shaped like mounds, they are watertight and safe from the beavers' enemies.

What does "playing possum" mean?

When people say somebody is "playing possum," they usually mean he is pretending to be asleep when he is really wide awake. The expression comes from one of the habits of the opossum, an animal about as big as a cat.

We don't see opossums very often because they sleep in the daytime and prowl around only at night looking for birds, fish, eggs, insects and fruit. When an opossum is suddenly surprised by a hunter, it pretends to be dead. This is a protection, for the animal seems to re-

alize that the hunter is looking for a live animal and won't bother with a dead one. And this is why we say people are "playing possum" when they pretend to be asleep.

Why does a cow keep chewing when it isn't eating?

Cows belong to a group of animals known as *ruminants*. These are animals that chew cuds and have a special kind of stomach for taking care of food that is hard to digest. Cattle, goats, sheep, deer and camels are all ruminants.

A cow first chews its food only enough to moisten it. Then it is swallowed and passed on to the first section of the cow's stomach. Here the food is stored, mixed and softened before passing to the second chamber where it is formed into little balls or cuds. Later, while the cow is resting, the cuds are returned to the mouth and chewed thoroughly. Again the food is swallowed, and this time it goes to a third section of the stomach where the moisture is squeezed out. Finally, it goes to the fourth section, or true stomach. Here the food is really digested.

What are antlers?

Antlers are the horns that grow on the heads of male members of the deer family, including elk, moose and caribou. The female caribou is the only American female deer that has them, but her antlers are much smaller than those of the male caribou.

Antlers are usually shed every winter, and in the spring new ones start to grow. At first they are just soft knobs covered with velvety skin. By fall the skin is gone, the antlers are tall and sharp, and the male is ready for the mating season. Then he fights other males, using his huge, bony, branched antlers.

Few shed antlers are found in the woods, because they are eaten by porcupines, mice and other small animals or they crumble from exposure to the weather.

Can camels go a long time without water?

Camels can go without water for a longer time than most animals, though not so long as some people think. Because they sweat very little, camels keep water in their bodies for a long time, using it very slowly. They can go for more than a week without water—especially if there are juicy plants to eat. When a thirsty camel finally gets a chance to drink, it often drinks as much as twenty gallons of water at one time.

It is also possible for camels to go for days without eating. They carry a pantry along with them in the form of excess fat stored in the solid hump on their back.

Deer

Moose

Elk

What is a ground hog?

Ground hog is another name for the common American woodchuck, a small animal related to the squirrel. It is a little less than two feet long and weighs about ten pounds.

In the fall the ground hog crawls into its hole for a long winter sleep. According to legend, it wakes up and crawls out again on February 2. If the day is sunny and the ground hog sees its shadow, it is supposed to be frightened. It crawls back into the hole to sleep through another six weeks of winter weather. If the day is cloudy and there is no shadow, the ground hog is supposed to stay out of his hole. This means there will be an early spring, and the ground hog is staying out to enjoy it. Of course the tradition of Ground Hog Day is just a harmless superstition, but people have fun talking about it.

Why do skunks give off an unpleasant odor?

When a skunk is angry or frightened, it shoots an oily spray into the air. This spray of bad-smelling liquid comes from two glands near the skunk's tail. If the liquid strikes the face of an animal, it burns and stings. If it strikes the eyes, it can cause temporary blindness. The unpleasant odor of the skunk is its greatest protection from enemies. It is almost impossible to remove the powerful smell from clothing.

Can porcupines shoot their quills?

Porcupines cannot shoot their quills, but the quills are loosely fastened and come out easily if the porcupine is touched by an enemy. Sharp barbs like fishhooks hold the quills deep in the enemy's flesh.

Usually the quills lie down flat next to the porcupine's skin, but they stand up straight when the animal is frightened or surprised. The tail of the porcupine is particularly full of loose quills, and the porcupine swings its tail freely when attacked by another animal.

Woodchuck

Skunk

Porcupine

About the Plant Kingdom

What were the first things to live on the earth?

The first things to live on the earth were plants—water plants. Along the shoreline, plants clung to the rocks. These plants were under the water when the tide was in, but they were exposed to the air when the tide was out. Gradually the water plants inched their way from the shore and became land plants. These were strange plants with no leaves. They had branching stems, part of which were underground to anchor the plant. What we know about these first land plants we have learned from fossils.

Will seeds grow after being kept for years?

A seed will grow if the embryo, the part that will become the new plant, is still alive. The length of time the embryo can stay alive waiting for favorable conditions to grow varies a great deal in different seeds. We have a new yardstick for measuring old things. It is called carbon 14.

When a scientist recently found a lotus seed, he used the carbon 14 test and discovered that the seed was 1,000 years old. He planted the lotus seed, and it grew and blossomed! This, of course, is very unusual, for most seeds will not grow if kept more than five or six years. Weed seeds, however, have been known to grow after forty years. Tales about seeds growing after being dug up from Egyptian tombs have not been proved true.

Lotus seed and blossom

What is the difference between a fruit and a vegetable?

We commonly think of apples, oranges and bananas as fruits, while such foods as spinach, potatoes and lima beans are usually called vegetables. But to a botanist, who studies plants scientifically, fruit is the seed or seeds of any plant, together with the parts which enclose them. For instance, string beans, eggplant and cucumbers all bear fruit—vegetable fruit. The seeds in this fruit grew from the plant's blossoms. We are eating vegetable fruits when we have cucumbers or eggplant for dinner. On the other hand, we eat the leaves of other vegetables such as lettuce and spinach, and we eat the roots or underground stems of beets, carrots and potatoes.

To most of us fruit must be sweet before we consider it truly "fruit," and it generally grows on trees, shrubs, vines or thick-stemmed plants.

What would happen if all the plants in the world died?

If all the plants in the world died, all animal life would eventually die too. At first we would miss the green grass and the leaves of the trees that shade us from the hot rays of the sun. Next we would miss food—juicy fruits, colorful vegetables and bread (for bread is made from two plants, wheat and yeast). Then, if we were still alive, we would begin to miss lamb chops, hamburgers, bacon and other meat, for the animals which supply these meats depend on plants for food. If the plants die, these animals must also die. We would soon die, too, since we would have nothing to eat.

What wild plants are good to eat?

It is foolish to eat any wild plant or berry unless you know positively what it is, for many are poisonous. Among those which grow wild but are good to eat are huckleberries, blackberries, raspberries and beach plums; the roots of Solomon's-seal, groundnut and pond lily; the leaves of plantain, dandelion and dock; the stems of wild asparagus and milkweed, and the bark of sassafras for tea.

What is chlorophyll?

Chlorophyll is the green coloring matter in plants. This remarkable substance makes it possible for plants to manufacture their own food. They can turn non-living matter into living matter. In the presence of sunlight, with water and carbon dioxide as raw materials, chlorophyll can accomplish a most remarkable chemical stunt. Sugar, starch and other elements can be made by the plant from these simple materials. In this respect, green plants have a great advantage over animals.

Why isn't a mushroom green like other plants?

A mushroom is a kind of plant called a fungus. These plants lack the green coloring matter of other plants. Since this green coloring matter (chlorophyll) is necessary for plants to make their own food, fungi are unable to carry on the food-making process. Therefore, mushrooms and other nongreen plants must absorb their food from dead wood or from soil which is enriched by decaying plants.

How does ivy cling to a wall?

Ivy clings to a wall by means of little sucker-like disks. These disks are attached by tendrils which are twining, threadlike parts of the plant. With these, the ivy can cling even to smooth walls. Ivy protects a well-built wall from the weather, but it may injure a poorly constructed wall by creeping in between the cracks.

Does moss grow on the north side of a tree?

Yes, moss is usually more apt to grow on the north side of a tree. The reason for this is that moss likes to grow in moist places on rocks and on tree trunks, and the north side is the side that strong sunlight does not strike. Thus moss usually thrives on the damp, dark side of the tree. However, in a thick forest moss may grow on all sides of a tree, because all sides are dark and shaded.

How can you tell poison ivy from other plants?

Poison ivy leaves are made up of three leaflets. Two of these leaflets form a pair on opposite sides of a stem, while the third leaflet is by itself at the end of the stem. There is a safety warning, "Leaflets three, let it be." This may not be good grammar, but it is good advice. Poison ivy can grow as a bush or a vine. It has shiny green leaves in summer; these turn a bright red in the fall. Its berries are yellowish white. Virginia creeper or woodbine is often confused with poison ivy, but has five leaflets instead of three. The irritation of poison ivy is caused by an oil in the plant.

Why is a cactus covered with spines or thorns?

The leaves of many plants lose several gallons of water each day by evaporation. But cactus plants would die if they lost even a few quarts of water a day, for they grow in deserts where water is scarce. Therefore cactus plants have developed special characteristics to preserve scarce water. Instead of having the usual kind of broad leaves, the cactus has modified leaves in the form of thorns. The thick green stems of the plant do most of the work that leaves would do. And they are able to store water. The spines or bristles, of course, protect the plant from desert animals that might eat the juicy stems as a source of water.

Poison ivy

Venus'-flytrap

Do plants ever eat animals?

Though we often forget it, all insects are members of the animal kingdom. And since there are certain plants that capture and eat insects, we can say that plants do sometimes eat animals. Among these insect-eating plants are the pitcher plant, the sundew and Venus'-flytrap.

The pitcher plant has tubelike leaves that hold rain water. Insects crawl down the tube, attracted by the sweet sticky liquid inside. But tiny hairs on the inside of the tube prevent the insects' escape. They slide down to the bottom of the tube where they are drowned and then digested by the plant.

The sundew has circular leaves with many hairs on the upper surface. Each hair has a drop of sticky liquid at its tip. In the sunlight these drops of liquid glitter like dew. When an insect is caught in the sticky fluid on the leaf, the hairs and the leaf curl in and trap it.

Venus'-flytrap is well-named, for it has a kind of hinge down the center of its leaves. There are sensitive hairs on the surface of the leaves, and when an insect lights on one of these hairs the two parts of the leaf close, trapping the insect inside.

Sundew

Pitcher plant

Do flowers sleep at night?

Flowers do not really go to sleep as we do at night, but many of them certainly do fold up. Look at a three-leaf clover during the day and notice that its leaflets are all spread out. Then look at it at night and notice that two leaflets have moved tightly face to face, and the third one is folded over them.

Many flowers have definite times for opening and closing. For example, morning-glory blossoms open in the morning and close when the sun becomes really hot. Four-o'clocks open in the later afternoon—around 4:00 P.M.—which is the hour when the California poppy closes. At sunset you can watch the evening primrose open as if by magic. These night-blooming flowers open when the light begins to fade. Other flowers open when the light gets stronger and the day gets warmer. Thus flowers do not actually sleep, but the blossoms or leaves often open and close on a regular schedule.

Does the pleasant smell of flowers help them any?

Yes, the pleasant smell of flowers does help them. It attracts insects and birds. When a bee, for example, goes deep into a morning-glory to get nectar to make honey, some of the yellow dust called pollen brushes off on its furry body. Then when the bee goes to another morning-glory plant, some of this pollen shakes off its body onto the second plant. In many cases this act of taking pollen from one flower to another is necessary before seeds can start to grow. Sometimes the wind carries pollen from one plant to another, but insects and birds are also important for the job. The flower attracts them by its pleasant odor and bright color.

Why does the dandelion turn white and fluffy?

The yellow blossom of a dandelion turns white and fluffy so that its seeds can float away in the breeze. Each little dainty white sail has a brownish seed attached to the bottom of it. This seed acts as an anchor. If all the seeds merely dropped to the ground below the plant, the seeds would be crowded together and the new baby plants would not have room to grow well. Therefore, the dandelion blossom turns fluffy and white, so that new dandelion plants can grow in favorable places.

What is the difference between a tree and a shrub?

Trees usually have one trunk; shrubs have several trunks or stems divided either at or near to the ground. Both are woody plants. Though we think of trees as being big and shrubs as being little, this is not always true. There are some trees, like the dogwood, which are quite small; and there are some shrubs, like the witch hazel, which are as tall as a small tree. Sometimes it is difficult to distinguish between shrubs and trees.

How do acorns turn into oak trees?

It certainly does fill us with wonder when we think of a tiny acorn becoming a mighty oak. The acorn is really a seed and has a baby plant inside, along with some food to help the plant get a start in life. The hard covering or coat protects the acorn until it lands in a favorable place where it can get good soil and moisture and start to grow. The growth, of course, is slow. A tiny seedling takes years to grow into a large oak tree. The tree will not bear acorns until it is about twenty years old.

Why do cherries and plums have pits?

It is the pit or seed, and not the fleshy part of the fruit, which is important to the growth of new cherry and plum trees. The delicious soft part of the fruit exists in order to give the living seed, or kernel inside the pit, a good chance to grow and make a new cherry or plum tree. Birds enjoy these fruits just as much as we do. Often they carry the fruit off and drop the pit in a place where it finds the right kind of soil and moisture to encourage the growth of the tiny plant inside the pit.

Do the rings of a tree stump tell its age?

Yes, the rings of a tree stump do tell its age, and by this method we know that some big trees are as much as 3,000 years old. When we look at the stump we see a series of dark and light rings. In the spring when the tree was getting plenty of water and sunlight, the light ring was formed and the trunk got wider. Later on toward the end of the summer the growing season slowed down. Three or four layers of dark cells were added, making a dark ring. Under favorable conditions, a dark ring for summer and a light ring for spring show a year's growth.

Why do leaves change color in the fall?

In the spring and summer the leaves are green because of the chlorophyll or green coloring matter that is inside them. This chlorophyll helps the trees to make their food with the assistance of sunshine, moisture and air. In the fall, when the trees have stored enough food for the winter, a ring of corklike cells grows across the leaf stem. These cells block the flow of water to the leaf blade. Without water, the leaf no longer makes food. The green chlorophyll disappears. Now the beautiful chemical colors which have always been present in the leaf can be seen. In addition, other new chemicals are formed, so we have the gorgeous crimsons, yellows and purples that we see in the fall.

How do we get maple syrup?

We get maple syrup from the sugar-maple trees. In the spring of the year a liquid called sap begins to run through the trees. This sap contains sugar produced by the tree. When the sap begins to run, a hole two inches deep is drilled in the bark. Then a little spout is driven in and a pail is hung to catch the sweet liquid.

At first the sap is watery and colorless, but after it is boiled down it turns into the thick, sweet maple syrup we eat on pancakes and waffles. If it is boiled even longer, the syrup forms into deli-

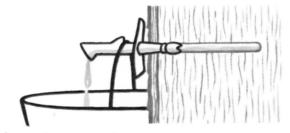

cious, hard maple sugar. Vermont is the famous maple syrup and maple sugar state, though New York and Ohio are also noted for them.

About Rocks, Minerals and Soil

What are fossils?

Fossils are the remains or indications of past plant or animal life on the earth. A fossil can be an actual bone, shell, tooth or part of a plant, or it can be the impression of such things left in rock. It can even be the original object replaced or filled in by mineral matter. Petrified wood is an example of such a fossil. The tracks or footprints of animals, or the borings of worms preserved in rocks, are also called fossils. Usually it is the hard parts of animals, such as bones, teeth and shells, that become fossils.

There are many ways in which fossils are formed. The remains of a dead animal may have been covered by the ooze of the ocean bottom, the mud of a shallow river or the shifting sands of a prehistoric desert. The soft parts of the creature decomposed or rotted away, and the tiny pores or holes in the bones gradually filled with mineral matter. This ancient mud, ooze or sand later hardened into limestone, shale or sandstone. Ages later, the fossilized remains of ancient plants and animals are found in these rocks. Fossils are generally found only in rocks that have built up in layers, called sedimentary rock.

Most plants and animals of course do not become fossils. They decompose when they die and leave no trace of themselves. That is why scientists search all over the world for fossils in order to piece together a picture of past life from the limited evidence that remains in fossil form.

How was coal made?

Coal was formed from trees which lived millions of years ago. These trees were not like our trees today; they were giant tree ferns. As these trees died, they fell into swamps and bogs. Other trees grew, died, and fell on top of them. Then the land sank, or perhaps the oceans rose. Mud and sand settled on top of the drowned trees. Through millions of years, these trees changed to a hard black rock called coal because of the enormous weight on them. Sometimes this coal is near the surface of the earth, sometimes men have to dig deep into the ground for it.

Where does dust come from?

Dust is made up of small particles, bits or pieces of almost anything. In a room, dust might be specks of cotton fiber, fine hair, pieces of wood, bacteria or even crumbs of dry paint. Outdoors, dust may come from crumbling rocks, plowed fields or dried earth. The wind picks up these tiny particles and carries them off. A large part of all ordinary dust is made up of mineral matter carried off by the wind.

What makes rock "icicles" form in caves?

The stone formations that look like icicles hanging down from the roofs of caves are called *stalactites*. They are formed when water drips very slowly from the top of the cave, carrying a mineral called calcium carbonate with it. Each drop stays in place long enough to let water evaporate, leaving behind a thin layer of the mineral. More drops reach the same spot, hang there until more water evaporates, and add another layer of the limey material. After thousands and thousands of drops do the same thing, an icicle-shaped spine hangs down from the roof of the cave.

Drops of water also fall to the floor of the cave, evaporate and leave calcium carbonate behind. Columns or "icicles" known as stalagmites gradually build *up* from the bottom of the cave.

Frequently stalactites and stalagmites join, forming solid columns between the cave's roof and floor.

What is quicksand?

Quicksand is a mass of extremely fine sand filled with so much water that it will not support weight. Usually a layer of clay or claylike substance beneath the sand prevents the water from draining away. The water keeps the grains of sand apart, keeps them from packing down hard. If a person steps into quicksand, it is just as though he stepped into water. He begins to sink.

Quicksand does not really pull people down, though it seems to—particularly if they thresh around. If you are caught in quicksand, act as though you are in water. Lie on your back with your arms outstretched. Rescuers can reach you by placing some flat object, such as a board or ladder, on top of the quicksand.

Digging foundations in or erecting buildings on quicksand can be a difficult problem for engineers.

What makes pebbles so smooth?

Pebbles are worn smooth by the action of water, wind and sand. In a babbling brook, for example, pebbles are bounced and jostled by the rapid movement of the water. At the same time the sand around the pebbles is churned up. The moving sand is just like sandpaper. It takes the rough surfaces off the small stones and makes them smooth.

Why do diamonds cost so much money?

Diamonds are expensive because they are so rare. Many people want these precious stones, and there aren't enough available to satisfy the demand. Diamonds are also expensive because of the high cost of locating, mining and cutting them. On account of their hardness, diamonds last longer than other gem stones; often they are used for cutting and grinding.

Great Star of Africa

Tiffany Canary Diamond

Star of the East

FAMOUS DIAMONDS

What are birthstones?

Birthstones are gems that are associated with special months of the year. In ancient times, people believed that gems had certain magical powers—both lucky and unlucky. Today people often wear jewelry associated with the month in which they were born. Following is a list of gems commonly accepted as the birthstones for each month of the year: January—garnet, February—amethyst, March—bloodstone, April—diamond, May—emerald, June—pearl, July—ruby, August—sardonyx, September—sapphire, October—opal, November—topaz, and December—turquoise.

How did the sand get on the seashore?

Sand is made from rocks. These rocks are broken up into tiny grains of sand by waves that pound the shoreline. The waves themselves are filled with sand, which the waves sometimes leave on shore. Ocean currents shift sand from place to place, often forming new beaches. These new beaches are sometimes made of sand from some distance away. Man himself can make a sandy beach by bringing in sand from another place.

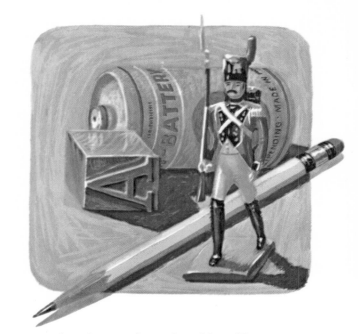

Is a lead pencil made of lead?

No, a lead pencil is not made of lead. It is made from a mixture of graphite and clay. Graphite is a soft black mineral made up of carbon. Soft-lead pencils, which make thicker, darker marks, have more graphite and less clay in them than do hard-lead pencils, which make sharp thin lines.

Real lead is a metal often used to make water pipes, toy soldiers, type for printing, storage batteries, and a covering for electric cables.

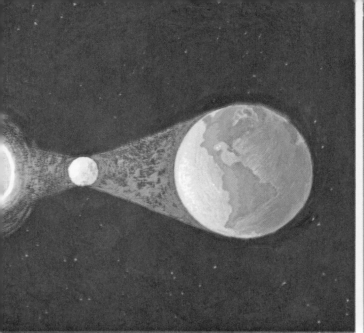

About the Oceans

Why do tides come in and go out?

Anyone who has lived near the seashore has noticed that the water along the shoreline slowly creeps higher and higher for six hours and then slips steadily down again for six hours. We call this rise and fall of ocean waters the tides.

The moon causes the tides by the pull it exerts on the earth. This force by which the stars and planets constantly pull at one another across space is called gravity. As the moon passes around the earth, it pulls the nearest water a little away from the solid earth beneath the ocean. The water is actually pulled into a bulge, and it begins to rise above the seashore. At the same time, the moon is pulling the hard core of earth away from the water on the opposite side of our planet. So a bulge of water rises there, too. In other words, high tides occur on opposite sides of the earth at the same time. Spring tides, or tides which are unusually high, are caused by the additional pull of the sun on the water, for at this time the earth, moon and sun are in a straight line. Neap tides, or lower tides, occur when the sun and moon pull at right angles.

Why don't the oceans freeze?

Most of our oceans never freeze because the water isn't cold enough. Ocean currents constantly shift warm water from areas of the world where it is summertime to areas of the world where it is wintertime. Then too ocean water is salty, and salt water has a lower freezing point than fresh water. The continual movement of the water also prevents freezing. Of course water in the polar regions—in the Arctic and Antarctic Oceans—*does* freeze during the winter months.

Why doesn't all the water in the ocean sink into the ground?

The bottom of the ocean is waterproof. It is made up of watertight rock or clay, through which the water cannot sink any lower.

What makes icebergs?

Icebergs are pieces of glaciers, great sheets of ice frequently found in the far north and the far south. Sometimes the edge of a glacier that is near water breaks off and floats away. This huge chunk of ice floating in water is an iceberg. It may float 2,000 miles before it melts. Icebergs are a great danger to ships, for most of the iceberg is under water and cannot be seen. In 1912 a giant passenger ship, the *Titanic*, hit an iceberg and more than 1,500 lives were lost. Today there is an Ice Patrol which reports icebergs.

Why are the oceans salty?

Rivers and streams are constantly flowing into the oceans, bringing with them salt, soil and other minerals. Where does this salt come from?

There is salt in rocks and in the soil. When rain falls on rocks it dissolves some of the minerals in them, particularly salt. The water washes into streams

and rivers, carrying away salt as well as dirt and stones. Then the water in the rivers takes over the job of wearing down the stones and setting free more salt. Salt and other minerals are also washed from the soil and carried off to the oceans by the rivers.

There is not enough salt in most rivers to make them taste salty, but after millions of years the salt carried to the oceans has made them quite salty. During all these years, ocean water has been evaporating, leaving the salt behind. This increases the saltiness of the oceans. There are beds of salt throughout the world, sometimes hundreds of feet thick, which were probably formed by the evaporation of ancient seas.

What makes waves?

The wind makes waves, just as you can make little ripples by blowing hard on a pan of water. Sometimes on a fair day you will see high, white-capped waves breaking against the shore. Yet you don't feel any breeze at all. Somewhere far away a wind must have pushed against the water and set it in motion. Wind is very powerful on water. Once it sets waves in motion they can travel thousands of miles.

The biggest waves are caused by earthquakes or volcanic eruptions under the ocean. These are called tidal waves and can cause tremendous damage when they wash up on the shore.

About the Stars, the

How far away is the sun?

The sun is about ninety-three million miles away from the earth. The earth, of course, goes around the sun. Since the path that the earth takes around the sun is not a perfect circle, the distance between the earth and the sun is not always the same. The path of the earth is a flattened oval called an ellipse.

How far away are the stars?

The sun is our nearest star and it is about ninety-three million miles away. The next nearest star is Alpha Centauri in the constellation of the Centaur. This star is more than twenty-six trillion miles away. Traveling at the rate of 186,000

miles a second, the light from Alpha Centauri takes more than four years to reach the earth. Thus we say that this star is 4.3 *light years* away. Some stars are hundreds of thousands of light years away from the earth.

Where does the sun go at night?

The sun appears to sink out of sight in the west every night. But actually the sun does not rise in the east and set in the west. It only appears to do so because of the movement of the earth. The earth is always turning, and it makes one complete spin every twenty-four hours. When our side of the earth faces the sun, we have daylight; when the spin of the earth takes our side of the earth away

Sky and the Weather

from the sun, we have night.

Man took many, many years to figure this out. Long ago people thought that the sun moved around the earth while the earth stood still.

Why don't the stars fall?

Stars are so far out in space that they are not affected by the gravity or pull of our earth. However, there is a gravitational attraction between these stars which holds them to their courses. If two stars come very close to each other, they may collide because of their own gravity, but this is extremely rare because the distances are so great.

Occasionally we see *shooting stars*. These objects are really meteors — not stars. Meteors are bodies made of iron and stone, traveling swiftly through space. When they enter the blanket of air around the earth, friction makes them light up. We call them shooting stars.

Do stars have five points?

The only stars with five points are the ones we draw, or cut out of paper and cloth, or make as ornaments out of glass and metal. Real stars are suns, like our sun, and they are ball-shaped. Sometimes when we look at the stars, rays of light seem to be streaming out in different directions. This appearance is caused by the earth's atmosphere as the light of the star passes through it.

Where do the stars go in the daytime?

Stars don't go anywhere in the daytime. They stay right where they are. We can't see them because the bright light of our "star," the sun, makes it impossible for us to see the fainter light of the faraway stars.

Why do stars twinkle?

The air in our atmosphere makes stars twinkle. Stars are suns, just like our sun, and they actually shine with a steady light. But the air between us and the stars makes them appear to be moving or shaking. Without a telescope we can see about 2,500 stars when we look at the sky on a clear night, but there are millions more stars we do not see. It has been said that there are more stars than there are grains of sand on all the beaches of the world.

Do people live on Mars?

Scientists don't believe that people could live on Mars, for there is not enough oxygen or water there to support human life as we know it. To us, Mars looks like a red star in the sky, and if we look at it through a telescope we can see dark green patches. These could be plants, for it is believed that plants do grow on Mars. Science-fiction writers like to make up stories about people from Mars. The writers choose this planet for their stories because it is a close neighbor of the earth, and its thin air makes it clearly seen and easily studied with a telescope.

What is the Evening Star?

The Evening Star is the first bright star we see in the evening. Actually it is not a star at all but a planet. Planets make no light of their own. Instead they reflect the light from our sun. To find out exactly what planet is the Evening Star on any particular date, look in the daily newspaper or in an almanac. Venus and Mars are the planets most frequently seen. Mercury, Jupiter and Saturn are others that are less frequently seen.

Why don't we fall off the earth?

We don't fall off the earth because of a very remarkable force called gravity. Gravity is the pull of the earth, the pull which makes everything on earth tend to fall to the earth unless it is held up by something.

What are the Northern Lights?

Northern Lights, also called the *aurora borealis*, are the beautiful long streamers or bands of light sometimes seen at night in the northern sky. They appear to shoot upward, constantly changing their positions and their brilliance. The lights may be white, yellow, green or red. It is believed they are caused by streams of tiny electric particles shot out by the sun during great magnetic storms. When these particles collide with the gases in the earth's atmosphere, they glow. The different gases in the air are the cause of the different colors. A similar light occurring in the southern hemisphere is called the *aurora australis*.

Cumulus

Cirrus

Nimbostratus

Why are clouds different on different days?

The clouds are different on different days because the weather is different. Clouds indicate weather. Their shapes and numbers are affected by differences of temperature in the atmosphere and by winds. When warm moist air rises from the earth, the water vapor cools up in the sky and turns into tiny water droplets. These droplets join with dust particles to become clouds.

There are several types of cloud forms. The *cirrus* are delicate fleecy, feathery clouds made up of ice crystals. They form high above all the other clouds, and are sometimes called "mares' tails." *Cumulus* clouds are huge, white, rounded, billowy masses with flat bases. Often they are "fair weather" clouds, but large numbers of them may mean rain. Sometimes they turn black and become thunderclouds.

Stratus clouds are straight layers of narrow bands, parallel to the horizon. These foglike clouds form about one hundred feet above the ground, usually when the air is still. *Nimbostratus* clouds are shapeless, dark gray rain clouds. They are packed with droplets of water which are colder and heavier than the warmer air around them, so the drops begin to fall, bringing rain.

What is the atmosphere?

The atmosphere is actually nothing more than the air that surrounds our earth. This atmosphere shields us from injurious rays of the sun. It also absorbs and holds some of the heat from the sun so that the earth is not too hot by day or too cold by night. More than one-fifth of the blanket of light gases we call our atmosphere is made up of oxygen. We need this gas if we are to keep alive. The atmosphere extends up at least 600 miles, but the higher up we go the thinner the air gets.

What is fog?

Fog is a cloud, but it is next to the ground instead of up in the sky. Fog is formed when warm moist air is cooled quickly. It is apt to form near a large body of water when the water is warmer than the land. As warm moist air rises off the water, it passes over the land and is quickly cooled. The moisture condenses, turns to tiny droplets of water, and forms a fog. London is famous for its fogs. Some cities are troubled with smog, which is a mixture of smoke and fog. On winter days you can make your own little fog or cloud by breathing your warm moist breath into the cold air.

Are snowflakes always different?

Yes, they are always different. If you look at snowflakes under a magnifying glass you will notice that no two flakes have exactly the same design. Though all of the flakes are six-sided, each delicate design differs from every other one. Scientists have examined millions of snowflakes to conclude this.

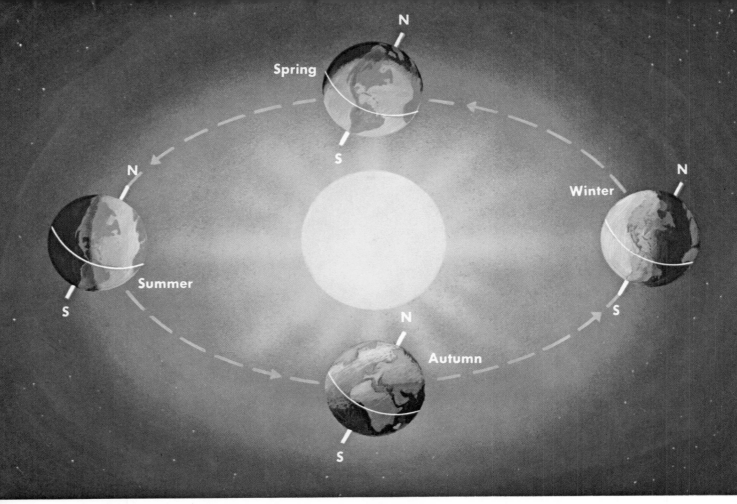

DIAGRAM SHOWING THE SEASONS IN THE NORTHERN PART OF THE WORLD, AND THE TILT OF THE EARTH AS IT REVOLVES AROUND THE SUN.

What causes the seasons?

Our seasons are caused by the fact that the earth is always tilted in the same direction as it goes around the sun. Look at the diagram and you will see how this works. For part of the year the North Pole is pointed toward the sun as the earth moves on its course. This means that the northern half of the earth is getting more direct sunlight. In North America, Europe and northern Asia, there is summer.

The other part of the year the North Pole is pointed away from the sun, and this brings winter to the same countries. The sun's rays are more slanted and less direct in winter than in summer.

Where does water go after a rain?

The heat of the sun takes some of the surface water back into the air as water vapor. But much water soaks into the ground. Plants take in some through their roots and later give it back to the air through their leaves. Some water keeps on sinking lower and lower into the earth until it strikes rock or clay and can go no farther. It may be carried along until it strikes a point where it can come out of the soil as a spring.

At very low depths, the heat of the earth may change the water to steam, thus causing geysers and hot springs. Of course much rain flows along streams to rivers and then to the sea. Some then goes back into the air as water vapor. Clouds form, and rain starts all over again.

What makes the wind whistle?

The wind itself makes no noise; we cannot hear an air current. Only when something is placed in the path of the wind do we hear it whistle and roar. When we are indoors, we hear the wind trying to force itself through windows and doors, into cracks and down the chimney. This swift-moving air sets many things to shaking and vibrating, and the vibrations give rise to various sounds and whistles.

What makes thunder and lightning?

Years ago Benjamin Franklin found out that lightning is really just a big spark of electricity. Storm clouds or thunderclouds contain a kind of electricity.

When this electrical charge becomes too great, a spark may jump from cloud to cloud or to the earth. The air around it is heated and explodes violently. This causes the sound waves which we call thunder.

What makes a rainbow?

After a shower you can see a rainbow in the sky if the sun is shining but the air is still filled with raindrops. Though sunlight looks white, it is made up of many colors—red, orange, yellow, green, blue, indigo and violet. The tiny raindrops can separate the sunlight into these different colors. If you stand so that the sun is behind you and the rain is falling in front of you, the rays of the sun will pass into the raindrops and you will see a rainbow. Sometimes little rainbows can be seen in the spray of a lawn sprinkler.

Index

WHY DON'T

How can ducks sit in the water without getting their feathers wet?

Do flowers sleep at night?

WHAT MAKES PEBBLES SO SMOOTH?

WHAT IS CHLOROPHYLL?

HOW CAN BIRDS FLY?

WHAT IS A

Where does the sun go at night?

How does a beaver make a dam?

HOW DO BEES MAKE HONEY?

WHAT WERE THE FIRST THINGS TO LIVE ON EARTH?

Can we hear the sea in a seashell?

HOW DOES IVY CLING TO A WALL?

How do fireflies light up?

WHY ARE THE OCEANS

WHY DO DIAMONDS COST SO MUCH MONEY?

WHAT